HOCKEY'S

BEST AND WORST

A Guide to the Game's Good, Bad, and Ugly

by

SEAN McCOLLUM

CAPSTONE PRESS
a capstone imprint

Sports Illustrated Kids Best and Worst of Sports are published by
Capstone Press, 1710 Roe Crest Drive, North Mankato, Minnesota 56003
www.mycapstone.com

Sports Illustrated Kids is a trademark of Time Inc. Used with permission.

Library of Congress Cataloging-in-Publication data
Name: McCollum, Sean, author.
Title: Hockey's best and worst : a guide to the game's good, bad, and ugly /
  by Sean McCollum.
Description: North Mankato, Minnesota : Capstone Press, 2018. | Series: Sports
illustrated kids. The best and worst of sports | Audience: Age 9 to 14.
Identifiers: LCCN 2017047195 (print) | LCCN 2017048696 (ebook) |
ISBN: 9781543506198 (eBook PDF) | ISBN 9781543506112 (hardcover)
Subjects: LCSH: Hockey—Miscellanea—Juvenile literature.
Classification: LCC GV847.25 (ebook) | LCC GV847.25 .M336 2018 (print) | DDC
  796.962—dc23
LC record available at https://lccn.loc.gov/2017047195

Editorial Credits
Nate LeBoutillier, editor; Bob Lentz and Terri Poburka, designers;
Eric Gohl. media researcher; Laura Manthe, production specialist

Photo Credits
Alamy: Paul Fearn, 4–5; AP Photo: 29, Paul Connors, 22; Getty Images: Bruce
Bennett, 13 (top), 15, 16, 27 (bottom), Dick Raphael, 26, Hyoung Chang, 23,
Sports Imagery/Ronald C. Modra, 25 (bottom), Steve Babineau, 12; Newscom:
Icon SMI/Freestyle, 9 (bottom), Icon SMI/IHA, 7, Icon Sportswire/Andrew Dieb,
13 (bottom), MCT/David L. Pokress, 11 (bottom), Reuters/Christinne Muschi,
21 (bottom), USA Today Sports/Marc DesRosiers, 25 (top), ZUMA Press/Nathan
Denette, 20 (top); Sports Illustrated: David E. Klutho, cover (all), 8, 9 (top), 14,
17, 18 (all), 19 (all), 21 (top), 24,28, Hy Peskin, 10, John Iacono, 27 (top), Robert
Beck, 11 (top), 20 (bottom), Tony Triolo, 6

Printed and bound in the United States of America.
010783S18

TABLE of CONTENTS

Dropping the Puck

The first indoor, organized ice hockey match was held, not surprisingly, in Canada. The contest took place on March 3, 1875, at Montreal's Victoria Skating Rink. Nine players from the same club skated on each side, unlike the six-stick lineup used today. There was little padding, no helmets, and body-blasting checks were still in the future. Up until then, the sport had been played with a ball. But with no high boards or glass to protect fans, organizers feared that the ball might cause injuries. For safety's sake, "a flat circular piece of wood" was used instead since it would not fly from the ice.

LET'S PLAY HOCKEY!

Skate forward nearly 150 years. Dion Phaneuf of the Toronto Maple Leafs takes a short pass as he leaves his team's defensive zone. Four strides later, he draws back his stick and blasts a slapshot on the Buffalo Sabres' goal. The puck, now made of hard rubber, definitely leaves the ice. It rockets over the shoulder of a well-padded goalie and hits the back of the net traveling more than 100 miles per hour.

No sport without an engine features more speed and power than NHL hockey. Action shifts from one end of the rink to the other in seconds. It also has its share of ice-smooth moves, wicked collisions, flying fists, and bloopers. You'll find some of the stories here — the good and the bad, the funny as well as the ugly.

CHAPTER 1

Offense & Defense

Wayne Gretzky

SCORERS

Hockey measures a scorer's skill by totaling goals plus assists. These points can come from slapshots blasted from the blue line or passes dished out from behind the net. They all count toward a player's point total.

GREATEST OF GREAT SEASONS

Wayne Gretzky, Edmonton Oilers, 1985–1986

There is Gretzky and everyone else. Of the top ten point-scoring seasons ever, eight belong to "The Great One." The 1985–86 season, though, was a 215-point masterpiece. He netted 52 goals to go with 163 assists! Most hockey experts doubt this NHL record will ever be topped.

Mario Lemieux

BEST!

Mario Lemieux, Pittsburgh Penguins, 1988–89 At 6-foot-4 and 230 pounds, "Super Mario" played like some kind of rocket-powered Zamboni, combining great speed and force. During the 1988–89 season, his best, that combo added up to 199 total points — 85 goals, 114 assists.

Phil Esposito, Boston Bruins, 1970–71 This was the year Esposito balanced 76 goals with 76 assists. Those 152 points crushed the record for that era.

FACTS AND STATS

In 1952, Bill Mosienko of the Chicago Blackhawks scored three goals in just 21 seconds. It remains the fastest hat trick in NHL history.

ONE-SEASON WONDERS

Sometimes skaters come out of nowhere. Then they go back there again.

Joe Juneau, Boston Bruins, 1992–93 In his second season, Juneau racked up 102 points — 32 goals plus 70 assists. He played 13 more seasons but never came close to those numbers again.

Blair MacDonald, Edmonton Oilers, 1979–80 His first year was special. Playing alongside fellow rookie Wayne Gretzky, MacDonald scored 94 points — 46 goals plus 48 assists. In four more years in the NHL, he didn't reach half those totals.

DEFENSEMEN

In the NHL, defensemen fall back to block hard-charging attacks. They throw themselves in front of flying pucks. They absorb a lot of punishment — and dish it out, too.

THE BEST OF THE BLUE LINE

Niklas Lidstrom

BEST!

Niklas Lidstrom, Detroit Red Wings
His steady leadership helped bring four Stanley Cup trophies to Detroit. He also collected the Norris Trophy, the NHL award for best defenseman, seven times. His best individual season: 80 points in 2005–06.

BEST!

Bobby Orr, Boston Bruins
Orr revolutionized the role of NHL defensemen. He attacked from anywhere on the ice. His relentless play earned him eight Norris trophies. His best season remains the NHL record for a defenseman: 139 points in 1970–71.

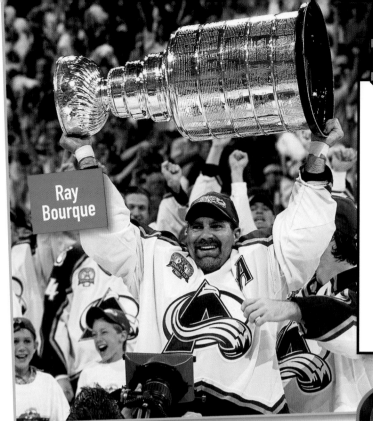

Ray Bourque

BEST!

Ray Bourque, Boston Bruins/Colorado Avalanche
Bourque played in 19 straight All-Star Games. In Colorado, he finished his career in style, lifting the Stanley Cup in 2000–01. He holds the record for defensemen in career goals (410) and career points (1,579). His best individual season: 96 points in 1983–84.

WORST!

Doug Gilmour, Montreal Canadiens
Though Gilmour ended up in the Hall of Fame, he is also remembered for the destruction of a penalty box in the 2002 playoffs. Furious at being sent to the sin bin, he slammed the door so hard the glass exploded.

SIN BIN SLAMMER

Dion Phaneuf, Calgary Flames In a 2005 match, Vancouver Canuck Jarkko Ruutu gave Phaneuf a hard check into the boards. Phaneuf threw down his gloves, ready for a fight. But before Phaneuf could throw a punch, Ruutu slickly tripped him with his stick. Fight over.

Doug Gilmour

CHAPTER 2

Goalies & Goons

THE BEST SEASONS IN THE CREASE

GOALTENDERS

Goaltenders must stay cool under fire. Action comes at them from every direction, even from behind the net. The masked man is always the last line of defense.

BEST!

Dominik Hasek, Buffalo Sabres

Known as "The Dominator," Hasek lived up to the nickname. His 1998–99 season, though, was his best of all. He had a save percentage of .937 — in other words, he blocked more than nine out of ten shots. He only allowed 1.87 goals per game and shut out opponents nine times.

Jacques Plante, Montreal Canadiens

For hockey gray-hairs, Plante was the greatest goalie to ever put on pads. His best season may have been 1955–56. He was a brick wall, allowing just 1.86 goals per game and compiling seven shutouts.

BEST!

Carey Price, Montreal Canadiens
Price owned 2014–15. He allowed an average of 1.93 goals per game, had a .933 save percentage, and kept the net empty during nine shutouts. He collected the Vezina Trophy for best goaltender and was also voted the NHL's Most Valuable Player.

FACTS AND STATS
In 2003–04, goaltender Brian Boucher strung together an NHL-record five straight shutouts for the Phoenix Coyotes.

WHOOPSIES!

Ken McAuley, New York Rangers
The season was 1943–44. World War II was raging and a lot of pro players traded their skates for combat boots. For the Rangers, that left semi-pro McAuley in the crease. He allowed 310 goals, a season record no goalie wants to match.

Vesa Toskala, Toronto Maple Leafs In a 2008 game, the New York Islanders cleared the puck from their own defensive zone. The shot bounded down the ice — and right past Toskala and into the net. It was a 197-foot goal.

Vesa Toskala

GOALIE MASKS

Starting in the 1960s, goaltenders wanted to keep straighter noses and more of their teeth. So they started wearing masks and then helmets. From that point on, goalie headgear has doubled as art.

COOLEST NHL GOALIE MASKS

Gilles Gratton, St. Louis Blues/ New York Rangers

When wings came charging toward Gratton, a roaring tiger glared back at them. Opponents said the that goalie himself had been known to growl.

BEST!

Jonas Hiller, **Calgary Flames** Maybe no goalie better represents his team name than Hayward. His helmet makes his head look as if it's on fire.

Ryan Miller, Vancouver Canucks

Miller's helmet resembled a face from a totem pole. It honors the native Haida people of Canada's Pacific Coast, where Vancouver is located.

WEIRDEST!

Gary Bromley, Buffalo Sabres/Vancouver Canucks
Bromley may have created the creepiest goalie mask. It was painted like a realistic skull and gave rise to his nickname: "Bones."

Pekka Rinne, Nashville Predators
Whatever the creature on his helmet might be, it looks ready to go hunting for some wings . . . or a center.

John Gibson, Anaheim Ducks
His Pac-Man-themed helmet sends a clear message: "Nom nom nom nom. I gobble up pucks."

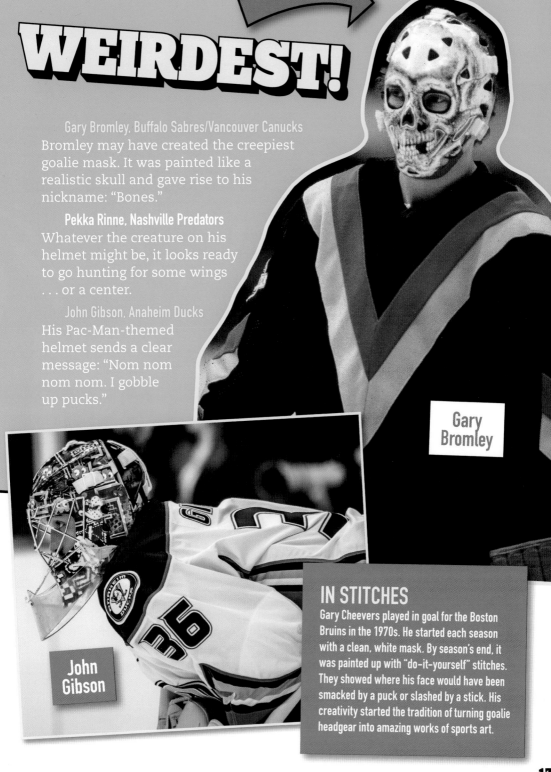

Gary Bromley

John Gibson

IN STITCHES
Gary Cheevers played in goal for the Boston Bruins in the 1970s. He started each season with a clean, white mask. By season's end, it was painted up with "do-it-yourself" stitches. They showed where his face would have been smacked by a puck or slashed by a stick. His creativity started the tradition of turning goalie headgear into amazing works of sports art.

ENFORCERS

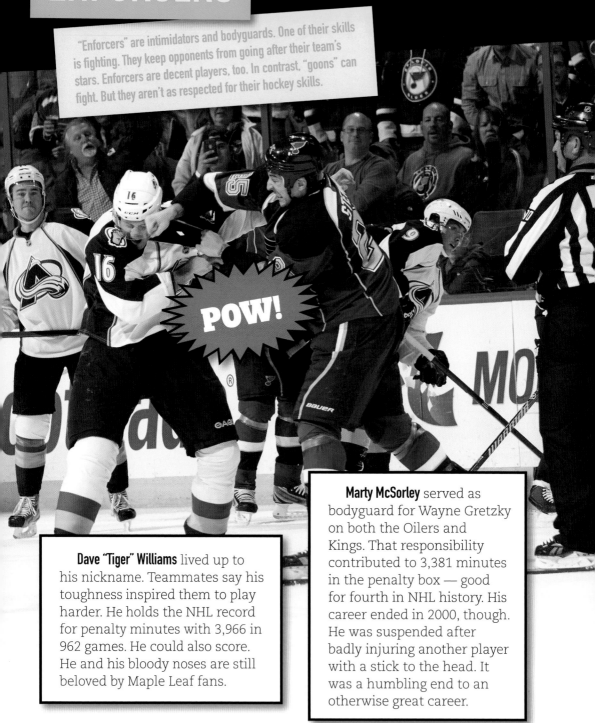

"Enforcers" are intimidators and bodyguards. One of their skills is fighting. They keep opponents from going after their team's stars. Enforcers are decent players, too. In contrast, "goons" can fight. But they aren't as respected for their hockey skills.

POW!

Dave "Tiger" Williams lived up to his nickname. Teammates say his toughness inspired them to play harder. He holds the NHL record for penalty minutes with 3,966 in 962 games. He could also score. He and his bloody noses are still beloved by Maple Leaf fans.

Marty McSorley served as bodyguard for Wayne Gretzky on both the Oilers and Kings. That responsibility contributed to 3,381 minutes in the penalty box — good for fourth in NHL history. His career ended in 2000, though. He was suspended after badly injuring another player with a stick to the head. It was a humbling end to an otherwise great career.

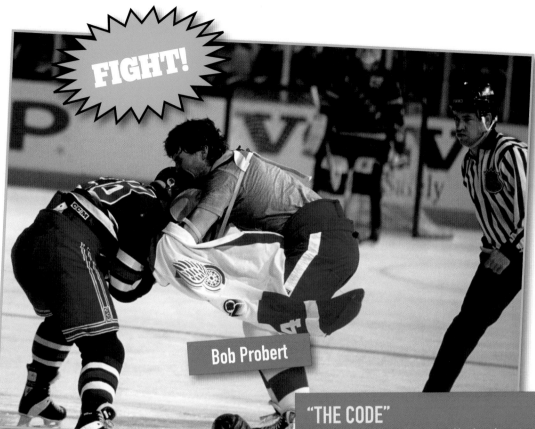

FIGHT!

Bob Probert

BEST!

Bob Probert, along with Joey Kocur, were Detroit's "Bruise Brothers" in the 1980s and 1990s. One of his main responsibilities was having the back of Red Wing all-star Steve Yzerman. Probert clocked 3,300 penalty minutes in his 15-year career.

FACTS AND STATS

Bob Probert died in 2010. Seven years later, Probert's wife put his ashes in the penalty box in Joe Louis Arena, home of the Red Wings.

"THE CODE"

Fighting has always been part of hockey. A sport this fast and furious triggers tempers. Defenders of hockey scraps say fights allow frustrated players to let off steam and protect teammates. Afterwards, the punchers usually end up cooling their skates in the penalty box.

NHL fighters follow unwritten rules to prevent serious injuries.

1. No sucker-punching. Both players know the fight is on.
2. Both players drop their sticks and remove gloves. Only fists are acceptable. Visors must come off so opponents don't cut their knuckles on the plastic.
3. The fight is over when one player stops punching, or the players fall to the ice. Then the refs move in to separate them.
4. Players shouldn't start a fight and then "turtle" — cover up to prevent getting hit. Taking punches as well as throwing them is a point of honor.
5. As a rule, players fight opponents of about the same size. Big guys don't pick on little guys. Ganging up on another player also breaks the code.

BRAWLERS

One-on-one fistfights are the rule in hockey. But sometimes bad blood between teams leads to bench-clearing brawls.

WORST!

WORST BRAWLS

Boston Bruins vs. New York Rangers, 1979 This brawl took place after the game. The Bruins had just won a close contest 4–3. A scuffle broke out between players, and then a Rangers' fan took a poke at a Bruin. Players and fans then went at it.

Philadelphia Flyers vs. Montreal Canadiens, 1987 This one started before the puck was even dropped. A couple of the Canadiens shot pucks into the Flyers's empty net during warm-ups, angering the Flyers. Wrestling matches turned into punches until almost all the players were mixing it up.

Philadelphia Flyers vs. Ottawa Senators, 2004 Tensions built as chippy play added up. Finally, it erupted into a rumble. Even the goalies went after each other. Officials handed out a total of 419 penalty minutes, an NHL record.

GENTLEMEN

Don't let the missing teeth fool you. Each year, the NHL awards the Lady Byng Memorial Trophy to the "most gentlemanly player."

BEST!

Pavel Datsyuk, Detroit Red Wings Datsyuk has enjoyed a long, successful career that includes two championships. He also owns four Lady Byng trophies and was twice voted the NHL's "Cleanest Player."

Pavel Datsyuk

THE GOOD SPORTS

Frank "Raffles" Boucher, Ottawa Senators/New York Rangers A star in the 1920s and 1930s, Boucher won two Stanley Cups and was inducted into the Hall of Fame. His opponents also respected him as a classy guy. He was awarded seven Lady Byng trophies in eight years.

FACTS AND STATS

The first hockey brawl? Apparently it came after the first organized hockey match in 1875. Some skaters went after the hockey players for wrecking the rink's ice.

CHAPTER 3

Fun & Fashion

LOOKING THE PART

MASCOTS

NHL's costumed cheerleaders started showing up in the 1980s. They have the job of firing up the crowd.

BEST!

Slapshot

Good hockey mascots try to strike a balance between fun and fierce. These beasties do it better than most.

Slapshot, Washington Capitals A bald eagle representing the U.S. capital is spot on.

Hunter, Edmonton Oilers Instead of an oil rig, the Oilers went with a Lynx mascot. Its kitty-cat grin looks like it could turn instantly into a spine-chilling snarl.

Gnash

Gnash, Nashville Predators
"Gnash," as in gnashing teeth, is a perfect name for a mascot with fangs like that.

MASCOT MAYHEM

Sometimes mascot pranks go hilariously wrong.

Harvey the Hound, Calgary Flames In a 2003 match, Harvey was dogging the Oilers bench. Oilers coach Craig McTavish reached up and yanked out Harvey's flapping red tongue.

S.J. Sharkie, San Jose Sharks Before a 1999 tilt, the San Jose mascot was being lowered from the rafters ... until he got stuck 40 feet in the air. As he dangled, the TV commentators made jokes at the shark's expense. "He's like a fish out of water," one said. A rope was finally lowered and Sharkie was pulled to safety.

Wild Wing, Anaheim Ducks To celebrate the Ducks' 1995 home opener, the team's mascot planned to jump a wall of fire in skates. The jump turned into a face-, er, bill-plant, and Wild Wing flopped into the flames. The duck was smoking but not roasted.

S.J. Sharkie

UNIFORMS

Hockey sweaters and their logos can bring out the pride in a team and its fans.

STYLISH SWEATERS

BEST!

Toronto Maple Leafs

Canada officially adopted its iconic red and white flag bearing a maple leaf in 1965. That was nearly 40 years *after* Toronto put white or blue leaves on its hockey team's sweaters.

Montreal Canadiens

The Canadiens' uniform is an all-time classic. It has done its duty for almost 100 years.

Boston Bruins Black, gold, and bold — the Bruins lineup comes at opponents like a swarm of big, bad bumblebees.

BEST!

WORST!

Some uniforms leave fans scratching their heads.

Edmonton Oilers, 2001–07
Even an oil-rig worker might not know what it is: A drill bit with a drop of oil on it.

New York Islanders, 1995–97
One *Sports Illustrated* writer suggested this logo featuring a sea captain looked more at home on a box of fish sticks than a hockey sweater.

Montreal Canadiens, 1912–13
When your regular sweater is nearly a hundred years old, you have to throw way back for your throwbacks. This one is from 1912–13. One opponent said the stripes on this version made him dizzy. The Canadiens wore them for exactly one game in 2009.

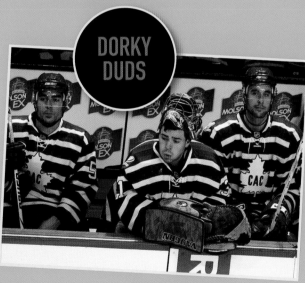

DORKY DUDS

FACT BREAK
One nickname for the Montreal Canadiens is the Habs. It's short for French settlers known as Les Habitants. French is the official language of Montreal, Quebec.

CHAPTER 4

Scoring & Celebrating

GOALS

A goal is always a cause for celebration . . . most of the time.

Alexander
Ovechkin

A PAIR OF THE GREATEST GOALS EVER

Seeing a favorite player put the puck in the net is among the biggest thrills for hockey fans. But some goals are just so amazing it doesn't matter who did it.

Denis Savard, Chicago Blackhawks, 1988 Taking the puck at his own blue line, Savard single-handedly deked and weaved through all the Oiler defenders, some of them twice. Finally, he got the shot off — and scored.

Alexander Ovechkin, Washington Capitals, 2006 Knocked to the ice, rolling onto his back, AND facing away from the net, he somehow kept the puck on his stick. He flicked it past the Coyotes' goalie for the score. In 100 years, hockey fans will still be watching this highlight.

BEST!

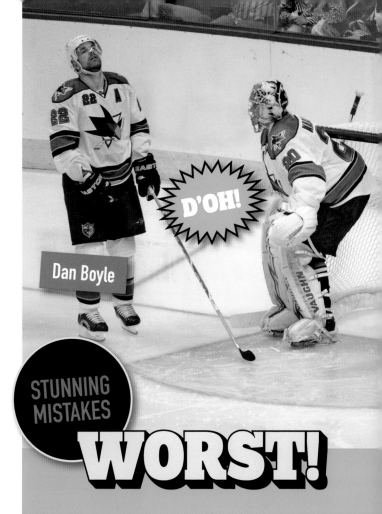

D'OH!

Dan Boyle

STUNNING MISTAKES

WORST!

There is no more embarrassing moment than helping your opponent by putting a goal in your own net in a hard-fought game.

Dan Boyle, San Jose Sharks, 2010 In a scoreless OT playoff game against the Avs, Boyle was in his own zone looking to pass behind the net. Instead, the puck shot past Boyle's own stunned goalie for the score, instantly ending the game.

Marc Bergevin, St. Louis Blues, 2000 This might be the oddest own-goal of all. Blues defenseman Bergevin gloved the puck out of the air as he skated toward his own net in a playoff game. He flipped it toward his own goalie, but instead it went into the net. The goal helped give the win to the Sharks, who went on to win the series in Game 7.

CELEBRATIONS

Hockey fans are filled with passion for the sport and their team. One of their traditions has been tossing stuff on the ice to celebrate. The NHL has banned the act, except when players score a hat trick. Then hats are acceptable.

Detroit Red Wings

In 1952 NHL teams needed eight wins total to hoist the Stanley Cup — two best-of-seven series. A couple crazy Red Wings fans tossed an octopus onto the ice. Its eight arms represented the eight wins needed. The Red Wings swept both series and flying octopi have been the Wings' good luck charm ever since.

Edmonton Oilers

In the 2006 playoffs, the Oilers were looking for some mojo to match the Red Wings' octopi. Fans started slinging steak onto the ice. (Edmonton's Canadian province of Alberta is famous for its beef.) Turf trumped surf, and the Oilers beat Detroit in six games.

CREATURES ON ICE

WHERE'S THE BEEF?

Andrew Hammond

EEK!

Ottawa Senators

Goalie Andrew Hammond came out of nowhere in 2014–15. When the team's starter was injured, Hammond took over the net. He proceeded to post a 20-1-2 record. Fans started calling Hammond "The Hamburglar" because he robbed opponents of goals. You can guess what they started flipping on the ice in his honor.

Florida Panthers

Before an October game in 1995, an unlucky rat was sneaking through the Panthers' locker room. Wingman Scott Mellanby snapped off a slapshot and killed it on the spot. That night he scored two goals. The story got out and fans started tossing plastic rats to celebrate success.

Which teams had the best seasons ever? Here are three that will always be part of the debate.

DREAM SEASONS

BEST!

Detroit Red Wings, 1995–96
The NHL record for most wins in a season? This team — 62-13-7 in the regular season. Their strength? The players didn't care how many goals they scored or minutes they logged as long as the team won. That dream season ended with a loss in the Finals. However, they brought the Stanley Cup home the next two years.

1976–77 Canadiens

Montreal Canadiens, 1976–77 The '76–77 Canadiens may've been the best NHL team ever. The Canadiens featured 10 future Hall-of-Famers that outscored opponents 440 goals to 194. They lost just two games in the playoffs and got out their brooms for the Stanley Cup, sweeping Boston in four.

BEST!

Edmonton Oilers, 1983–84
This team, led by Wayne Gretzky, set the NHL record for goals in a season, and finished an NHL-best 57-18-5 in the regular season. They mounted a balanced attack, with four players topping 100 points. They also stole the Stanley Cup from the New York Islanders, who were trying for their fifth title in a row.

NIGHTMARE YEARS

WORST!

These worst records all belong to first-year franchises. A team has to start somewhere.

Washington Capitals, 1974–75: 8 wins, 67 losses, 5 ties.

Ottawa Senators, 1992–93: 10-70-4.

Kansas City Scouts, 1975–76 In their first two seasons they won just 27 times in 160 games. Eventually they moved to New Jersey, where they had more luck as the Devils.

1974–75 Caps

STANLEY CUPS

Only one team takes home The Cup when the season comes to an end.

BEST!

These championship battles lived up to the hype!

BEST FINISHES

Colorado Avalanche vs. New Jersey Devils, 2001
Down 3 games to 2, the Avalanche staged a comeback. The gritty goaltending of Patrick Roy led the way. He allowed just one goal in the final two games and was named series MVP.

Washington Capitals vs. New York Islanders, 1987
These two teams battled to seven games, and then came "The Easter Epic." Game 7 went into four overtimes and lasted nearly seven hours. The Islanders finally scored the winning goal in the early hours of Easter Morning.

Pittsburgh Penguins vs. Detroit Red Wings, 2009 This series was a rematch from the year before. Game 7 was an instant classic. Detroit just missed sending it into overtime when Penguins' goalie Marc-Andre Fleury made a diving stop.

WORST!

You win some, you lose some. But this loss stung worse than any before or since.

DISAPPOINTED!

Detroit Red Wings vs. Toronto Maple Leafs, 1942

The Red Wings won the first three games. Then the skates fell off. The Maple Leafs took Game 4 (4-3) ... Game 5 (9-3) ... Game 6 (3-0) ... and Game 7 (3-1) to rip off four straight wins and claim the Cup. It remains the best Stanley Cup comeback — or worst collapse — in NHL history. It all depends on who you were rooting for!

BEST!

Members of the 1941–42 Maple Leafs

ABOUT THE AUTHOR

Sean McCollum is a long-time sports fan who proved to be hopeless on any kind of skate. With a hockey career out of the question, he turned to writing for young people. He has written more than 40 books for kids, tweens, and teens on everything from Theodore Roosevelt to werewolves to the world's fastest racecars. You can find out more about Sean's work at his website: www.kidfreelance.com.

GLOSSARY

brawl — a rough or noisy fight or quarrel that includes multiple fighters

classic — used to say that something has come to be considered one of the best of its kind, or an example of excellence

crease — area around or in front of the goal

era — period of time that is associated with a particular quality, event, person, etc.

hat trick — three goals scored by one player in a single game

own-goal — a goal that a player accidentally scores against his own team

revolutionize — to change something completely

sweep — to win all of the games in a series

trumped — to do better than an opponent in a contest or competition

Zamboni — machine used to resurface ice for skating

READ MORE

Frederick, Shane. *Six Degrees of Sidney Crosby: Connecting Hockey Stars.* North Mankato, Minn.: Capstone Press, 2015.

The Editors of Sports Illustrated. *Hockey: Then to WOW!* New York: Time, Inc., 2017.

The Editors of Sports Illustrated. *Sports Illustrated Hockey's Greatest.* New York: Time, Inc., 2015

INTERNET SITES

FactHound offers a safe, fun way to find Internet sites related to this book. All of the sites on FactHound have been researched by our staff.

Here's all you do:

Visit *www.facthound.com*

Type in this code: 9781543506112

INDEX